A WOMEN'S HISTORY BOOK

When I Close My Eyes

NAREMEEN SALEM

Palmetto Publishing Group

Charleston, SC

When I Close My Eyes... a Women's History Book

First Edition

Printed in the United States

ISBN-13 9781641116671

ISBN-10: 1641116676

Dedication

To my niece, Noor (*my* light*),
may I see you
on one of these pages someday.

I dream
that I am
as **brave** as
Anne Frank.

Anne Frank, a Jewish teenager, wrote a diary of her family's two years in hiding (1942–44) during the German occupation of the Netherlands in World War II, and the book—which was first published in 1947, two years after Anne's death in a concentration camp—became a classic of war literature, personalizing the Holocaust.

Berenbaum, M. (2019, June 18). Anne Frank.
Retrieved from https://www.britannica.com/biography/Anne-Frank

I dream
that I am
as **courageous**
as **Malala.**

Already at eleven years of age **Malala Yousafzai** fought for girls' right to education. After having suffered an attack on her life by Taliban gunmen in 2012, she has continued her struggle and become a leading advocate of girls' rights.

Winner of the Nobel peace prize "for their struggle against the suppression of children and young people and for the right of all children to education."

The Nobel Peace Prize 2014. (n.d.).
Retrieved from https://www.nobelprize.org/prizes/peace/2014/yousafzai/facts/

I dream
that I am
as **dominant** as
Serena Williams.

Serena Williams is an American professional tennis player who has held the top spot in the Women's Tennis Association (WTA) rankings numerous times over her stellar career.

I dream
that I am
as **fierce**
as **Beyoncé.**

Beyoncé Knowles is a multi-platinum, Grammy Award-winning recording artist who's acclaimed for her thrilling vocals, videos and live shows. She is also the first female artist to debut at No. 1 on the Billboard 200 with her first five studio albums.

Beyoncé Knowles. (2019, July 16).
Retrieved from https://www.biography.com/musician/beyonce-knowles

I dream that I am as **creative** as **Freda.**

Frida Kahlo was a central figure in the Neomexicanismo Art Movement in Mexico which emerged in the 1970s. Her art has been called folk art due to traditional elements and some call it Surrealist though Kahlo herself said, "They thought I was a Surrealist, but I wasn't. I never painted dreams. I painted my own reality." In May 2006, her self-portrait Roots sold for US$5.6 million dollars setting an auction record for a Latin American piece of art.

Frida Kalo Facts. (n.d.).
Retrieved from https://www.fridakahlo.org/frida-kahlo-facts.jsp

I dream
that I am
as **loving**
as **Ellen.**

Ellen DeGeneres hit it big as a stand-up comedian before starring on her own sitcom, Ellen. In 1997, she came out as gay, and became a staunch advocate of LGBTQ rights. She has been the host of her own award-winning talk show, The Ellen DeGeneres Show.

Ellen DeGeneres. (2019, October 8).
Retrieved from https://www.biography.com/media-figure/ellen-degeneres

"I think adults out there need to know they're doing the same thing. It's not just kids. There are adults out there that are bullying, and they need to be kind."
—Ellen DeGeneres

I dream
that I am
as **adventurous**
as **Amelia Earhart.**

Amelia Earhart was an American aviator, author and women's rights activist. She was the first woman to fly solo across the Atlantic. Her disappearance in 1937 during an attempt to fly around the world is a mystery that continues to intrigue people worldwide.

Amelia Earhart: Biography & Disappearance. (n.d.).
Retrieved from https://www.livescience.com/29363-amelia-earhart.html

I dream
that I am
as **awesome**
as **Michelle Obama.**

Michelle LaVaughn Robinson Obama is a lawyer, writer, and the wife of the 44th President, Barack Obama. She was the first African-American First Lady of the United States. Through her four main initiatives, she has become a role model for women and an advocate for healthy families, service members and their families, higher education, and international adolescent girls education.

Michelle Obama. (n.d.).
Retrieved from https://www.whitehouse.gov/about-the-white-house/first-ladies/michelle-obama/

I dream
that I am
as **ambitious**
as **Susan B. Anthony.**

Susan B. Anthony, an American women's rights activist, devoted her life to racial, gender, and educational equality. One of the most famous women in American history, she played a prominent role in the women's suffrage movement; the 19th Amendment, which gave women the right to vote, is named in her honor.

5 Important Facts about Susan B. Anthony · Career Training USA · InterExchange. (n.d.).
Retrieved from https://www.interexchange.org/articles/career-training-usa/5-facts-about-susan-b-anthony/

I dream
I am a **leader**
such as
Harriet Tubman.

Harriet Tubman was the most famous conductor of the Underground Railroad. In a decade she guided over 300 slaves to freedom; abolitionist William Lloyd Garrison thought she deserved the nickname "Moses". She worked hard to save money to return and save more slaves. In time she built a reputation and many Underground Railroad supporters provided her with funds and shelter to support her trips.

Short Biography. (n.d.).
Retrieved from http://www.harriet-tubman.org/short-biography/

I dream to be the **first** woman President of the **United States** of America.

About The Author

Naremeen Salem is an English Language teacher in Philadelphia, Pennsylvania. She teaches a very diverse group of young learners in an urban school setting. She herself attended Philadelphia public school's as a child, graduated from Temple University with her bachelors in Early Childhood Education, and received her Master's in TESOL and Literacy from Holy Family University. Naremeen is a first-generation college graduate with Palestinian immigrant parents. She lives with her husband and 2-year-old son in Philadelphia.

CPSIA information can be obtained
at www.ICGtesting.com
Printed in the USA
BVHW020150280120
570708BV00017B/407